Self-Scoring
Emotional
Intelligence
Tests

Mark Daniel

INTRODUCTION BY Victor Serebriakoff

STERLING

Published by Sterling Publishing Co., Inc.
387 Park Avenue South, New York, NY 10016

© 2000 by Mark Daniel
This 2000 edition published by Sterling Publishing Co., Inc.,
by arrangement with Constable & Robinson Ltd.

Distributed in Canada by Sterling Publishing
c/o Canadian Manda Group, 165 Dufferin Street,
Toronto, Ontario, Canada M6K 3H6

Distributed in the United Kingdom by GMC Distribution Services,
Castle Place, 166 High Street, Lewes, East Sussex, England BN7 1XU

Distributed in Australia by Capricorn Link (Australia) Pty. Ltd.
P.O. Box 704, Windsor, NSW 2756, Australia

ISBN: 978-0-7607-2370-8

35 34 33 32 31 30 29 28

For information about custom editions, special sales, premium and
corporate purchases, please contact Sterling Special Sales Department
at 800-805-5489 or specialsales@sterlingpub.com.

Disclaimer:
These tests are not meant to replace a professional examination. The accepted view is
that the only valid test is an individual test administered by a qualified professional.

INTRODUCTION

In 1995, psychologist Daniel Goleman published his groundbreaking book, *Emotional Intelligence*. It immediately became a worldwide bestseller, because, where IQ tests often seemed irrelevant and much of psycho-analytical literature incomprehensible and concerned with extreme conditions, *Emotional Intelligence* addressed our responses to everyday social interactions and challenges.

EQ – or Emotional Quotient – is not just about mastering emotions and conditioned reflexes for personal benefit or for the greater good. The emotionally intelligent person acknowledges emotion in himself and in others and uses it appropriately. All reflexes and resultant emotions are there for a good reason, but, while anger, depression and so on have their purposes in nature as in modern life, they have a tendency to feed themselves and so grow out of all proportion, or, if acted upon without intelligence, to have inappropriate and disproportionate consequences.

Emotional intelligence, then, consists not in denial of emotion but in sense of proportion, in the ability to reason or distract oneself from emotional folly or obsession. The emotionally intelligent famously know how to defer gratification, but they also know how and when to let their hair down and have a good time.

It is perfectly possible, therefore, that a model of restraint may be impossible to live with because a partner cannot find emotional common ground, to be an apparent saint yet phenomenally destructive, or to be the life and soul of the party whilst harboring deep, unacknowledged, but nonetheless damaging insecurities.

EQ, unlike IQ, cannot be gauged across the board nor simply divided into "good" or "bad," "right" or "wrong." It is true that EQ, far more than IQ, ordains success, but success in different fields means different things to different people. For this reason, this book is divided into separate sections designed to test your EQ in specific regards and to identify strengths and weaknesses.

Emotional intelligence can be trained. It might be argued, indeed, that "training," as opposed to teaching, by definition deals with emotional intelligence, in that it intends to replace one set of reflexes with another, or, rather, to give the new set of reflexes priority – though not total supremacy – over the other. Anyone honest enough to acknowledge identified areas of weakness can profit from these tests.

Victor Serebriakoff 1999

CONTENTS

THE TESTS

How to take the tests
There are no right or wrong answers. Answer impulsively and quickly. Circle the answer that comes closest to your own emotional response, then turn to the key at the end of the book and total your score, then you can interpret your scores.

ARE YOU EMOTIONALLY LITERATE?

Emotional intelligence is not merely about controlling emotional responses for one's own benefit and that of others. It is also about using emotion where suitable. Emotion is, after all, at the heart of that sincerity which reassures, persuades and affords confidence; emotion triggers flight or fight, sometimes appropriately; emotion is necessary if we are to cope, for example, with bereavement; emotion can lie at the source of our greatest joys. The emotionally intelligent are like parents to their emotions, acknowledging their needs, loving them, indulging them where appropriate, encouraging their creativity yet restraining them from foolish, destructive or discourteous behavior. To extend the metaphor, the emotionally intelligent are neither of the school which believes that emotions should be repressed – "seen but not heard," nor of that which would allow the little darlings to "express themselves" freely to the discomfort or dismay of others. Emotional literacy with regard to others can only be learned by reference to the ABC of one's own emotions. If, therefore, you are not at ease with your own emotions, you will find it hard to relate to others and to respond appropriately to them.

Circle the answers that come closest to your own emotional response; then turn to page 23 to interpret your score.

1. Your child, in direct contravention to your orders, runs into the busy road. You pull him/her back and:
    a) smack or shake him/her?
    b) master your emotions and explain why this was not a good idea?
    c) master your emotions and resolve upon subsequent punishment?

2. You then:
    a) tell the child off and threaten him/her with dire punishment?
    b) apologize and explain that mommy/daddy was frightened?
    c) burst into tears?

3. It annoys you to:
    a) have to make the most of your physical attributes at work?
    b) see others making the most of their physical attributes at work?
    c) see others unkempt or sloppily dressed at work?

4. You are infuriated with your partner. Do you:
    a) refuse to speak for days?
    b) swear, and go for a walk?
    c) plot revenge?

5. Your parent/parent-in-law is nagging, sarcastic and interfering. Your principal feeling is:
    a) resentment?
    b) resignation?
    c) pity?

6. Grief is:
    a) a necessary and salutary process?
    b) something which time will heal?
    c) a blight on your life?

7. Does worry serve a purpose?
    a) sometimes?
    b) never?
    c) always?

8. You are outraged by a newspaper story. Do you:
    a) rant at your friends/family?
    b) write a letter to the newspaper?
    c) become depressed?

9. Is your anger:
    a) a spur to change?
    b) a spur to hurt or destroy things?
    c) destructive of yourself?

10. Time is, above all:
    a) the great healer?
    b) the great destroyer?
    c) to be ignored or vanquished?

11. A violent crime is, to you:
    a) "a reflection of a general trend in society?"
    b) "an isolated, tragic case from which we can draw a lesson?"
    c) "an outrage about which something should be done?"

12. You like music to be, primarily:
    a) soothing?
    b) exciting?
    c) deeply moving?

IS YOUR SELF-IMAGE POSITIVE OR NEGATIVE?

We can at once be at ease with our emotions yet have a negative self-image, which, in terms of emotional intelligence, is like having a car but no fuel. Emotional intelligence is a means to personal tranquility, but such tranquility cannot coexist with self-despite, nor be maintained without communicating itself to others. Without a positive perception of ourselves, it is hard to be frank about our emotions, either with others (an essential tool in communication) or with ourselves, and we are thus prevented from analyzing, controlling and using them to good effect. It is of vital importance that we come to accept and like ourselves. Often the otherwise emotionally intelligent have allowed others – parents or partners – to convince them of a fundamental untruth: that they are somehow less valuable than any other member of the human race. This colors every emotional response. Liking ourselves and accepting our emotions does not mean giving our emotional responses free rein or espousing the doctrine that emotion justifies foolish or irresponsible actions. It does mean freeing ourselves from the confines of prejudice by recognizing in others impulses which we acknowledge in ourselves. The emotionally intelligent can at once understand the criminal because his motives are familiar, and judge and condemn him where necessary. Such ambivalence would be impossible with negative self-image and hatred of all too human frailties in ourselves.

Circle the answers that come closest to your own emotional response; then turn to page 24 to interpret your score.

Look at the following numbers. How do you immediately define them?
1. ①/one
    a) solitary, lonely?
    b) erect, proud?
    c) slim, tight?

2. ⑧/eight
    a) plump, jolly?
    b) fat, squat?
    c) dual, divided?

3. ⑦/seven
    a) elegant, relaxed?
    b) magical, mystical?
    c) slimy, sidling?

4. Children are most likely to succeed if they read:
    a) fairy tales?
    b) educational books?
    c) history?

5. Nudism is:
    a) beautiful or funny?
    b) disgusting or pathetic?
    c) it depends on the bodies?

6. How would you describe your body?
    a) unsatisfactory, ugly?
    b) far from perfect, but it does its job and attracts the people that matter?
    c) pretty darned good, thanks?

7. You see a beautiful member of your own sex. Do you feel:
    a) admiration?
    b) envy?
    c) scorn?

8. You bear a given name, but always have the choice to use another. If you have not done so, how do you feel about that name?
    a) I don't like it/hate it.
    b) I like it. It suits me.
    c) It doesn't really suit me, but I can't be bothered to change.

9. Involuntary bodily functions inspire:
    a) admiration, wonder?
    b) indifference?
    c) revulsion?

10. Your hero/heroine is/was:
    a) a feisty fighter?
    b) a victim who fought back?
    c) first and foremost a giver, and a star?

11. Life is:
    a) a bitch?
    b) a party?
    c) a battle to be enjoyed?

12. War is:
    a) a sorry, inevitable consequence of beloved human nature?
    b) a terrible crime?
    c) when we are truly alive?

ARE YOU AN EXTROVERT OR INTROVERT?

Introspection is, of course, an important component of emotional intelligence. We cannot relate to others and order our responses until we have examined our own virtues and failings. At the same time, an excess of introversion is selfish and isolationist and prevents creativity and effective social interaction. The excessively extrovert, however, deter and intimidate, and frequently substitute reactive intelligence with a fixed, bluff, confident self-image which conceals inner bewilderment.

Circle the answers that come closest to your own emotional response; then turn to page 25 to interpret your score.

1.   You are in a foreign country where you have but a smattering of the language. You want to buy an avocado, a lamb chop and a bottle of wine. Do you:
   a)   look up the right words in the dictionary and the phrase book?
   b)   ask for the goods in your mother tongue and assume that someone will be found who speaks it?
   c)   have a go at the host country's tongue, coupled with mime and farmyard noises?

2.   You hear mocking laughter from a corner as you walk across a room. You:
   a)   scowl defiantly?
   b)   inspect your clothing and scurry for cover?
   c)   draw yourself to your full height and smile broadly at the people laughing?

3.   Which most closely describes your mood of an early morning?
   a)   tetchy and impatient?
   b)   jolly and encouraging?
   c)   tranquil and purposeful?

4.   When you order clothes made, you order them:
   a)   smaller than your current size, because you are going to lose weight?
   b)   your current size?
   c)   with plenty of 'growing-room'?

5.   Would a partner's infidelity:
   a)   make you feel inadequate?
   b)   sadly show up his/her inadequacies?
   c)   sadly demonstrate that your relationship is inadequate?

6.   You are about to enter a crowded room, full of chattering, glittering people, alone. Do you:
   a)   resolve to sneak in and skulk in the corner until you see a familiar face?
   b)   assure yourself that you are as bright and attractive as anyone else there?
   c)   have absolutely no problem. A couple of drinks, and you'll take the party by storm?

7. A person who knows you well ignores your greeting and passes you without a word or smile. Do you:
   a) assume that he/she was preoccupied?
   b) take offense and brood?
   c) pursue and ask him/her what you have done wrong?

8. The couple in the apartment above yours makes love noisily during the night. Do you:
   a) feel resentful and bang on the ceiling?
   b) bury your head under the pillow?
   c) awake your partner and whisper that you might as well make a similar noise yourselves?

9. Christmas is:
   a) hell on earth.
   b) a magical time.
   c) tough, but worth it.

10. New Year is:
    a) hell on earth.
    b) an excuse for a wild party.
    c) an excuse for a quiet night in.

11. The intolerable thing in a relationship is:
    a) indifference.
    b) infidelity.
    c) rows.

12. Your boss holds a door open for you. You:
    a) walk through with a grateful smile.
    b) say, "no, please, after you."
    c) walk through, saying, "thank you very much."

ARE YOU INDEPENDENT?

Intellectual independence, loyalty in the face of peer-pressure, a refusal to abandon friends or principles when battered by the tide of fashion, keeping your head when all about you are losing theirs, and blaming it on you – all these are admirable qualities. They afford you a core, a moral touchstone, when things become ramshackle and chaotic. They also prove a "rock" for others. Although at times the less sturdy may be alienated by your independence of spirit or you are branded eccentric or "old-fashioned," those same critics will flock to you when their lives fall apart.

    A human being, however, is not a rock, but an organic, growing, constantly metamorphosing, sensate being. No one inspires less confidence or respect than the bigot (be he or she liberal and trendy, or conservative and nostalgic) who formed opinions at an early age and has refused ever since to listen, to learn, or to change. Equally the person whose opinions, tastes and beliefs change by the minute, depending on the company he or she is in, does little to inspire the confidence of others. Indeed, harmless as his or her motives (which might even be unconscious) – and these are all too often an effort to be liked through agreeing with others' views – they become distrusted.

Circle the answers that come closest to your own emotional response; then turn to page 26 to interpret your score.

1.   Friends and people whom you respect assure you that a certain sort of music is wonderful. You hear it once and dislike it. Do you:
    a) pretend to like it?
    b) openly avow your distaste?
    c) keep an open mind and listen to it again?

2.   Your best friend's husband/wife is flaunting an affair with a younger partner. Friends find this amusing. Do you:
    a) advise the offending party at least to be discreet?
    b) tell your best friend?
    c) join in the secret laughter?

3.   Sex is for you:
    a) a way of asserting yourself and gaining pleasure?
    b) a way of surrendering yourself and giving pleasure?
    c) a way of attaining all of these?

4.   A crowd roars its approval of a speech. Do you:
    a) automatically mistrust the crowd-impulse?
    b) get caught up in the crowd's approval?
    c) buy the text and go home to consider?

5.   How often do you leave the phone off the hook or the cell phone switched off?
    a) often – on holiday, in restaurants, in the bath etc.?
    b) never – it could be important?
    c) seldom – you like to keep in touch?

6. In a restaurant, you are served food which is cold, over-salted or plain revolting. Do you:
   a) summon the waiter and quietly ask to have the dish replaced?
   b) say nothing for fear of a row?
   c) say nothing until the end of the meal, then insist on a reduction in the bill?

7. Solitude for a full day or evening is:
   a) intolerable without the radio/television/telephone?
   b) a delight, a chance to think and to recharge the batteries?
   c) intolerable, inducing a sense of failure?

8. Your partner is invited on a company junket abroad. You are:
   a) delighted for him/her and looking forward to seeing non-mutual friends?
   b) resentful. You will head down to the travel agent on your own account?
   c) outwardly supportive, but storing up recriminations for future use?

9. "Worry is a horse which you whip but only circles." You worry:
   a) never?
   b) only when it can lead to solutions?
   c) all the time?

10. You are hard-pressed for money. A bill arrives in the mail. Do you:
    a) leave it unopened until you can pay it?
    b) open it and fall into depression?
    c) open it and instantly telephone the sender to propose terms of settlement?

11. A lover is:
    a) a necessity?
    b) a luxury?
    c) a part of the furniture?

12. Music is:
    a) to be heard while doing other things?
    b) to be listened to alone?
    c) to create an atmosphere when with others?

WHO IS IN CHARGE, THE CHILD OR THE ADULT?

We are, of course, the consequences of our genes, our experiences and our education, the sum of our past emotions – all of which to some extent ordain our emotional responses in the here and now. Many irrational fears or dislikes, for example, have their roots in "long-forgotten" traumas or even dreams. The notion of "maturity" frequently presupposes a stolid self-reliance founded upon common sense, and independence from such residual influences, but such resilience can be dearly bought, at the cost of the vulnerability essential to empathy. On the other hand, no one wants to hitch his or her wagon to the star of an eternally whimpering infant. The balance is a delicate one, and, once again, depends upon emotional intelligence, which distinguishes between those emotions that can constructively be entertained and others that, unchecked, are destructive or debilitating.

Circle the answers that come closest to your own emotional response; then turn to page 27 to interpret your score.

1. A close friend dies. You are – honestly – most concerned at:
    a) your own loss?
    b) his/her family's loss?
    c) the circumstances of the death?

2. Illness in yourself, preventing work or fun, is:
    a) a damned nuisance, but inevitable.
    b) devastating and unfair?
    c) someone else's fault?

3. A friend is in the hospital. You:
    a) take fruit and flowers and stay a good long time.
    b) take magazines, letters and photographs and visit briefly.
    c) cannot stand hospitals and stay away.

4. Depression makes you:
    a) attack or sulk at your partner?
    b) eat/drink too much?
    c) go shopping?

5. You are not invited to be godparent to the child of someone whom you had thought to be your dearest friend. You:
    a) send the child a loving letter and an expensive present?
    b) say nothing, and assume that your friend's reasons will become clear in due course?
    c) take offense and vow that you will have nothing more to do with your friend?

6. Stood up for a date, you:
    a) get defiantly drunk/defiantly pick up someone else?
    b) shrug and return home to a good book?
    c) persist in phoning the offender way into the wee small hours?

7. You are most likely to cry at:
   a) happiness, romance, love triumphant?
   b) rejection, death, disaster?
   c) sacrifice, renunciation, courage?

8. Which quotation most closely reflects your views?
   a) "Love conquers all?"
   b) "Men were deceivers ever"/"Frailty, thy name is woman?"
   c) "It is better to have loved, and lost, than never to have loved at all?"

9. You hear that a close friend or lover has spoken ill of you. Do you:
   a) assume that the message-bearer is malicious or mistaken?
   b) assume that the friend was misunderstood or under pressure?
   c) launch into a similar attack on the friend/lover?

10. Your lover proposes a new sexual game – dressing up, say, or role reversal. You:
    a) think it ridiculous and refuse?
    b) go along with the experiment, but feel embarrassed and worried?
    c) go for it?

11. Stuck in a traffic jam, you:
    a) fume, seethe, curse?
    b) fret about the people at your destination?
    c) take the opportunity to think, sing, play?

12. Your child or a child in your care is afraid of something which you know to be perfectly harmless – a spider, say. Do you:
    a) talk to him/her, play spider games, make light of the fear?
    b) become exasperated, and urge him/her not to be silly?
    c) hide the spider or whatever and pretend that it was never there?

ARE YOU A FOLLOWER OR A LEADER?

There is room on this earth for only so many compulsive leaders, and nature provides, thank God, a strictly limited number. Not only are such natural leaders unable to tolerate so much as a glimpse of a competitor – even within the family or in trivial social contexts – but few of us have the constitution to withstand the constant, unrelenting internal pressure which impels such people. Compulsive leadership, like genius, is closely related to, and can often become, madness; like genius, it seems to spring from deep insecurity, often without apparent cause; like genius, it can achieve remarkable things, but is dangerous when thwarted, impossible to live with, and, because it is that most dangerous and stupidest of things – a general, or absolute principle – there is no limit to its cravings. Henry VIII, who had syphilis, with its compulsive monomania, was unwilling (or unable) to see anything in his way as he strove for an heir. Thousands died in pursuit of his cause, yet he would not be checked. Interestingly, these people have temporary victories only. Trees adapt to the power of the elements, and, through their flexibility they endure. Napoleon and Hitler were defeated not by others like them, but by those who recognized the need for give and take. In the Duke of Wellington and Winston Churchill, they met men who did not believe themselves insuperable but acknowledged their own "weaknesses" – the proof that we are human – and were comfortable with them. Their people followed them for that reason.

The compulsive leader, then, is no object of aspiration. He will burn up fast, and find no mourners at his pyre. Of independent-thinking, self-disciplined, creative leaders, however, there is no shortage. Most of them, it must be said, spring from classes already established in this book, and established in childhood – independent, pensive, empathetic, spiritual – ready and willing to care where caring is apposite, yet, when called into action, ready and willing to act at once for their own good and that of their friends and followers. Such people care greatly for the feelings of others, not least because the feelings of others are central to their marketing and efficient management, but are not dependent upon the approval of others, and can, where necessary, sentence a beloved employee or friend to (professional, if not actual) death.

And then there are the followers, the deputies. A good deputy will in turn lead, but will not carry ultimate responsibility. He or she should remain a deputy, for, if promoted beyond his or her natural position, he or she could hurt many people and ultimately fail. This is not to say that the deputy is inferior to his/her master. Simply that he/she does not possess the desire or the talent to swim deepest rivers, climb highest mountains, etc., alone. It is of the first importance that we decide now which role is ours. The good deputy may become rich and valued. The poor leader is buying him- or herself an express ticket to hell. If your life's work is hell, you're not winning . . .

Circle the answers that come closest to your own emotional response; then turn to page 28 to interpret your score.

1. On vacation, you:
    a) remain at all times in contact with the office?
    b) phone once or twice a day to pick up messages, but otherwise devote yourself to your family/friends?
    c) forget work?

2. You arrive home after work, on average:
    a) so soon as you can after working hours end?
    b) in plenty of time for a drink or a bath before dinner?
    c) just in time for dinner?

3. You dress for work:
    a) with elegance and comfort in mind?
    b) to impress/inspire confidence?
    c) fashionably?

4. Your principal leisure activities:
    a) are gregarious?
    b) are solitary but accompanied by noise (computer-games/background music/television etc.)?
    c) are solitary and largely silent?

5. Someone jeers at you or pokes fun at you. Your first response is:
    a) soothing/humorous?
    b) firm but cool?
    c) angry?

6. Someone jeers or pokes fun at a subordinate in his/her absence. Your first response is:
    a) soothing/humorous?
    b) firm but cool?
    c) angry?

7. If someone working for you arrived consistently late, you would:
    a) have him/her in for a stern warning?
    b) enquire as to his/her circumstances and health?
    c) not mind much so long as his/her work was OK?

8. Who should be working hardest in the workplace?
    a) the boss?
    b) the managers?
    c) the bluecollar workers?

9. You want your children, above all, to:
    a) have every material advantage?
    b) have a good education, then they're on their own?
    c) find their own roles and be happy?

10. You read, mostly:
    a) books and magazines about management/business/your trade?
    b) biographies?
    c) fiction?

11. If you won the lottery, you would:
    a) give large sums of money to family and friends?
    b) invest the money and use small sums out of income to enable family and friends?
    c) keep the lot for yourself and your descendants?

12. At weekends, you read which page of the newspaper first?
    a) social/opinions/sports?
    b) financial?
    c) arts?

ARE YOU MAKING THE MOST OF YOURSELF AT WORK?

There are many ways of regarding work. For some, it is a necessary evil, for some, a raison d'être, for others a social duty, for an unhappy few, an escape from the emotional burdens of home life and self. Whether you are dealing with family or colleagues, suppliers or traders, government departments, bosses or domestic staff, you are bound to encounter frustrations. The workplace is in some regards a place of surrender. You may try to lay down clear ground-rules for conduct, but they are seldom going to be heeded with any great consistency at work. Everyone at the workplace has a different "agenda," different terms of reference, different aims and ambitions, and is afflicted by different moods which you have little time to assess on a day-to-day basis. You may have to speak, in essence, a hundred different languages to a hundred different people in any one day. One way out of this – the coward's way – is to maintain a consistent persona which in time becomes taken for granted. The consistently grumpy, autocratic manager, say, the consistently proper, precise bureaucrat, the consistently driven, demanding, impatient wheeler-dealer or the consistently disapproving, inhumanly correct parent – all are unassailable within their armor, but such armor also renders the wearer insensitive to others, sometimes with devastating effect on morale and seldom, in the long run, to the benefit of the wearer. At the same time, the workplace cannot become a touchy-feely group-counselling center nor can every hard luck story be heeded. How, then, can you make the most of yourself at work, be that work in the office or at home; how can you win success, and how can you enjoy your work? It seems strange to some that these are the same questions, but emotional intelligence can put a spring into the step as you set off for work, can make the workplace productive and pleasurable and can win rapid success.

Circle the answers that come closest to your own emotional response; then turn to page 29 to interpret your score.

1.   How many hours' leisure do you have in every twenty-four hours?
      a) 4–6
      b) 7–9
      c) 10–16?

2.   A colleague is in a filthy mood which is affecting others at the workplace. Do you:
      a) demand that he/she pulls him/herself together?
      b) buy him/her a cup of coffee and tell him/her about some problem of your own?
      c) ask him or her directly what the trouble is?

3.   A good salesman:
      a) sticks rigorously to techniques as trained?
      b) uses every trick in the book to make a sale?
      c) is sincere and principled?

4.   You feel that your immediate superior is working against your interests and those of the company. He/she will not listen to your ideas. Do you:
      a) go over his/her head to his/her superior?
      b) quietly canvass the views of your colleagues?
      c) work on resentfully and keep the tenuous peace?

5. Someone yawns whilst you are addressing a meeting. Do you:
   a) assume that he/she is not interested or committed?
   b) assume that you are being boring?
   c) not link the two things at all?

6. A colleague, equal in status to yourself, although outwardly a hard worker, is not pulling his/her weight or is undermining the team spirit. Do you:
   a) express your feelings to him/her?
   b) express your feelings to his/her colleagues and superiors?
   c) lead by example and insist on his/her participation in your projects?

7. You are in what seems to you a dead-end job, unnoticed, your work taken for granted. Do you:
   a) enroll in a training course, motivate your colleagues, then, if you see no further prospects, look for a new job?
   b) look for a new job?
   c) complain to your supervisors, then, if you see no improvement, threaten to look for a new job?

8. A client/colleague is angry and impatient and wants results now, regardless of procedure or rules. Do you:
   a) retire behind a screen of regulations and formality?
   b) snap back that you are doing the best you can?
   c) agree that procedures are infuriating and try to find out why he/she is so agitated?

9. Teamwork is:
   a) a good way of bringing on and instructing the less able?
   b) a darned nuisance. You know how to attain your aims and prefer to work alone?
   c) the key to good management?

10. A bright young prodigy rockets up the promotion ladder. Do you:
    a) resent him/her and suspect nepotism/unseen favors?
    b) seek to make friends with and to learn from him/her?
    c) sink into depression and sense of inadequacy?

11. You are negotiating a deal. You approach the negotiations:
    a) ready to listen?
    b) having identified an upside and a downside and determined to demand the maximum and concede the minimum?
    c) knowing what you want and determined to get it?

12. The person with whom you are negotiating a deal refuses to budge from an untenable position but simply bombards you with the same demands. You:
    a) thank him/her for the time, but say that you can see no point in continuing this dialogue and leave the meeting?
    b) take up your position and bombard right back?
    c) continue to attempt to make him/her listen?

IS YOUR RELATIONSHIP IN DANGER OF "FLOODING"?

Daniel Goleman derives the term "flooded" from psychologist John Gottman to describe the sort of relationship in which aggressive and defensive reflexes have become a way of life between two or sometimes more people. Associations with past hurts, slights and indignities blinds the "flooded" to their partners' virtues and strengths, deafens them to the voice of reason. Continued "flooded" relationships destroy the health, psychological no less than physical, of all within their orbit, but the flooded are unable to break free of the dreadful cycle. Offense is taken to the most inoffensive remarks; a careless glance is taken for a sneer; natural habits which had once seemed acceptable, even lovable, become irritating almost beyond bearing. This is the loneliest state on earth – far, far worse than isolation – in which your dearest friend and closest companion has become your bitterest enemy, and you have no one to turn to but the cause (as you see it) of your ills. Sometimes flooding has an identifiable trigger – an infidelity, perhaps, which one party has forgiven in theory, but cannot forget in practice, alcoholism, or deceit. In some ways, such cases are more readily addressed and dealt with than those which creep up on a relationship like a bad habit, inexplicable, unnoticed at first, interrupted by ever shorter idyllic interludes and, finally, enveloping every waking – and some sleeping – moment. Rows in any relationship are inevitable – even, some would say, healthy.

Circle the answers that come closest to your own emotional response; then turn to page 30 to interpret your score.

1.   Your partner is:
a)   always difficult and demanding?
b)   almost never difficult and demanding?
c)   impossible, but OK really?

2.   You are:
a)   forgiving, tolerant, understanding?
b)   passionate, devoted, courteous?
c)   impossible, but you love him/her.

3.   What does the future hold for the two of you?
a)   tough times, but a lot of fun together?
b)   tough times, and you have no faith that things will change?
c)   roses all the way?

4.   You have financial worries. He/she caresses you on the sofa. You think:
a)   "Why does he/she always choose the wrong moment?"
b)   "That's a good idea. Let's take time out from those boring bills?"
c)   "I owe it to him/her to snap out of it?"

5.   She/he admires a member of the opposite sex on the street. You feel:
a)   amused?
b)   furious?
c)   here we go again . . . ?

6. He/she says, "Darling, we have got to talk . . ." You think:
a) "Not more of his/her wheedling or browbeating."
b) "Uh-oh, what's gone wrong?"
c) "Just what I was going to say."

7. He/she proposes a quite outrageous sexual experiment, bred of a formerly shared fantasy. You:
a) react violently, claiming that you went along with the fantasy only at his/her behest?
b) ask for time to consider, and hope that it will be forgotten?
c) think that this might be rather fun?

8. He/she raises an objection to your plans. You say:
a) "Oh, well, forget it."
b) "Typical. You can't accept any idea which is not your own."
c) "Hang on a second, darling. Let me think about this . . ."

9. He/she is always:
a) enigmatic, confusing, lovely?
b) self-centered, self-absorbed?
c) variable, surprising?

10. Loneliness is:
a) impossible. You have your own company?
b) a daily experience?
c) being without your partner?

11. He/she has:
a) always let you down?
b) never let you down?
c) always amused you, so what the hell?

12. He/she is untidy/lazy/inconsiderate:
a) as a general rule?
b) occasionally?
c) never?

INTERPRETATION OF YOUR SCORES

Are you emotionally literate?

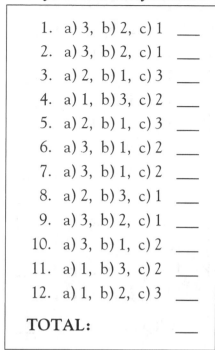

1. a) 3, b) 2, c) 1 ___
2. a) 3, b) 2, c) 1 ___
3. a) 2, b) 1, c) 3 ___
4. a) 1, b) 3, c) 2 ___
5. a) 2, b) 1, c) 3 ___
6. a) 3, b) 1, c) 2 ___
7. a) 3, b) 1, c) 2 ___
8. a) 2, b) 3, c) 1 ___
9. a) 3, b) 2, c) 1 ___
10. a) 3, b) 1, c) 2 ___
11. a) 1, b) 3, c) 2 ___
12. a) 1, b) 2, c) 3 ___

TOTAL: ___

12–19: You are ill-at-ease with your emotions, and thus, for all your apparent good intentions, you take refuge in "appropriate" responses, often of bland submissiveness. If you cannot confront your emotions honestly, acknowledging that they are, however violent, valid, you can only repress them or simulate a proper response rather than turning them to constructive use. Remember that all emotions have been felt before and are, to a greater or lesser extent, common to all humans. Repressing them results in mental and physical illness, fiercely held convictions which are not emotionally true, and often moralistic dogmatism.

20–27: Your robust attempts to master your emotions are praiseworthy but frequently ill-judged and unsympathetic. You defend yourself from "unworthy" emotions by simulating appropriate responses, but you tend to give rent-free space in your head to people and things which were better considered, understood and consigned to the emotional data-bank for subsequent use. Try *allowing* emotions, even emotions which seem unworthy – anger, fear, frailty, depression, etc. – into harmless contexts such as when listening to music or watching films, explore them and acknowledge them. They are part of the armory of wisdom.

28–36: You have no problem in accepting and using your emotions when appropriate, while imposing restraint on destructive impulses. You are comfortable with your natural responses where they serve their turn and know how to channel their useful physiological consequences to best effect.

Is your self-image positive or negative?

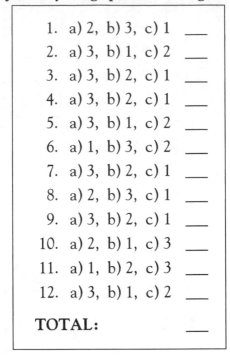

1. a) 2, b) 3, c) 1 ___
2. a) 3, b) 1, c) 2 ___
3. a) 3, b) 2, c) 1 ___
4. a) 3, b) 2, c) 1 ___
5. a) 3, b) 1, c) 2 ___
6. a) 1, b) 3, c) 2 ___
7. a) 3, b) 2, c) 1 ___
8. a) 2, b) 3, c) 1 ___
9. a) 3, b) 2, c) 1 ___
10. a) 2, b) 1, c) 3 ___
11. a) 1, b) 2, c) 3 ___
12. a) 3, b) 1, c) 2 ___

TOTAL: ___

12–18: Come on. You aren't really that bad. Look at yourself in the mirror. Marvel at the way in which every minute, complex part of you functions, then tell me that you are not remarkable and wonderful. And all this dislike of others is really founded upon nothing more than dislike of yourself. Beautiful, rich, successful people can still feel pain, you know, and insecurities. Your smile or enthusiastic help could make you valuable even to them. Disapproval and dislike should be reasoned and specific. Where it is general, it speaks of mistrust of your own nature not of others'.

19–27: Whoah, there. You certainly accept what you think you are, but are you sure that that image tallies with the real you – fallible, frail, uncertain, mortal man or woman? Your aggression and assertiveness seem to speak rather more of poor self-image and of confidence in a projection. Whereas those in the category 12–18 will have the humility to do something about it, however, you may find rather more difficulty in developing an accurate appreciation of yourself. The projection, after all, is popular enough, and you never need to consider all those inconvenient little flaws which make you human. This in turn makes you intolerant of the same flaws in others.

28–36: You do not have to assert yourself – which is to say, defend yourself – in order to inspire confidence. Your positive self-image, founded upon the reality, not a projection, will readily communicate itself to others. You appear to be "happy in your own skin." It is contagious.

Are you an extrovert or introvert?

1.	a) 2,	b) 3,	c) 1	___
2.	a) 3,	b) 2,	c) 1	___
3.	a) 3,	b) 2,	c) 1	___
4.	a) 3,	b) 1,	c) 2	___
5.	a) 2,	b) 3,	c) 1	___
6.	a) 2,	b) 1,	c) 3	___
7.	a) 1,	b) 2,	c) 3	___
8.	a) 3,	b) 2,	c) 1	___
9.	a) 3,	b) 2,	c) 1	___
10.	a) 2,	b) 3,	c) 1	___
11.	a) 1,	b) 2,	c) 3	___
12.	a) 1,	b) 3,	c) 2	___

TOTAL: ___

12–19: You seem to have attained a balance between self-love and self-awareness, assurance and introspection. You are confident, yet not so overweeningly so as to have banished sensitivity towards others. You are resilient yet considerate, and well-equipped to survive emotional turmoil because you are in touch with your own inner self.

20–27: Your timidity is a handicap, your mistrust of yourself almost now a conditioned reflex, inhibiting you from emotionally intelligent communicative responses. You need to remind yourself that there are many people who could benefit from your good offices, you need to count your doubtless many achievements and blessings, you need to look at the many people less fortunate, weaker, stupider, and less attractive than yourself and thus train your own emotional intelligence to lead you to take responsibility and to make a positive contribution to your society, your environment and your own welfare. If your want of self-worth is a consequence of an unappreciative partner or family, look to the outside world in order to exercise your emotional intelligence.

28–36: Quite the life and soul of the party, confident, opinionated, tetchy, and ebullient, you may fool yourself, but we have our suspicions. Do you notice other people? Are their emotions even related to yours? You have programmed yourself to react confidently and assuredly to any circumstance, but it is time that you considered your own frailties, however well disguised, and related them to those of others.

Are you independent?

```
 1.  a) 1,  b) 3,  c) 2   ___
 2.  a) 2,  b) 3,  c) 1   ___
 3.  a) 3,  b) 1,  c) 2   ___
 4.  a) 2,  b) 1,  c) 3   ___
 5.  a) 2,  b) 3,  c) 1   ___
 6.  a) 2,  b) 1,  c) 3   ___
 7.  a) 3,  b) 2,  c) 1   ___
 8.  a) 2,  b) 3,  c) 1   ___
 9.  a) 3,  b) 2,  c) 1   ___
10.  a) 3,  b) 1,  c) 2   ___
11.  a) 1,  b) 2,  c) 3   ___
12.  a) 3,  b) 2,  c) 1   ___
```

TOTAL: ___

12–19: It is sad to be so dependent upon others yet so aggressive and moody as to alienate most people upon whom you might depend. Resentment, futile worrying, dwelling upon grievances and in need of constant external stimulus, your very need makes you a victim, and so the cycle goes on. Only you can break it. Your temperament, of course, is in part innate, but the emotionally intelligent "born worrier" starts by recognizing that, while worrying has a purpose, it has its place; that love is wonderful, but that, when it is not around, there is more to life; and that stubbornness, though splendid when applied to arduous tasks, has no merit whatsoever when applied to ordinary social interaction. Compartmentalize. Devote set times to resolving the causes of worry, other times to reading and thus becoming other people . . . Above all, devote time to silence, to walking or meditating. Make a life for yourself, and so recognize that others have their own lives, and cannot devote them to you.

20–27: Communicative, gregarious when necessary, yet unafraid of silence and solitude, you would seem to be sufficiently confident at once to assert yourself without insecure aggression where suitable and to be "happy in your own skin" even when alone.

28–36: Oh, you seem fiercely independent, assertive and constantly busy, but it would seem that, in your own way, you are as tied up in yourself – and dependent upon others' responses to you as favorable or unfavorable – as the eternal victim. It is time to take a holiday from the non-stop assertion of self. After all, if you are content with your self, why does it need asserting? Independence, true independence, may be concerned with others' welfare, but not with others' opinions.

Who is in charge, the child or the adult?

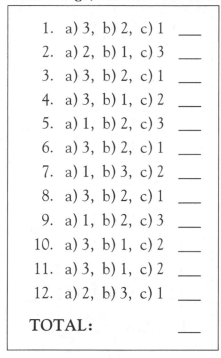

1. a) 3, b) 2, c) 1 ___
2. a) 2, b) 1, c) 3 ___
3. a) 3, b) 2, c) 1 ___
4. a) 3, b) 1, c) 2 ___
5. a) 1, b) 2, c) 3 ___
6. a) 3, b) 2, c) 1 ___
7. a) 1, b) 3, c) 2 ___
8. a) 3, b) 2, c) 1 ___
9. a) 1, b) 2, c) 3 ___
10. a) 3, b) 1, c) 2 ___
11. a) 3, b) 1, c) 2 ___
12. a) 2, b) 3, c) 1 ___

TOTAL: ___

12–19: Nervous, sentimental, conscientious and timorous, and convinced that the world has somehow singled you out for maltreatment and misfortune, you have retained, paradoxically, much of the self-importance of the child. The dice really are not specially loaded against you, and there is no call to worry so much about the consequences of your actions or about others' views of you. Life is for living, and you can change things for the better if only you can count and appraise your achievements and those who depend on you or would appreciate your help.

20–27: Blithe and confident, and quite ready to be playful and irresponsible where appropriate, you would seem to have reconciled the needs of the child – to be loved and nurtured – with the adult role of lover and nurturer.

28–36: It is amazing how many people consider themselves adult because they are robust, demanding, fretful and noisy, although these are all characteristics of the tantrum-throwing, attention-seeking, insecure infant. The insecurity manifested in docility and worry by the group in 12–19 is, in you, manifest in impatience and vociferous insistence on being acknowledged and getting your way. Cultivate real confidence, which can be quiet and unobtrusive, and learn to play where play hurts no one. Life is short, and your dignity is not diminished by taking things easy.

Are you a follower or a leader?

1.	a) 3, b) 2, c) 1	___
2.	a) 1, b) 2, c) 3	___
3.	a) 2, b) 3, c) 1	___
4.	a) 3, b) 1, c) 2	___
5.	a) 2, b) 3, c) 1	___
6.	a) 3, b) 2, c) 1	___
7.	a) 3, b) 2, c) 1	___
8.	a) 3, b) 2, c) 1	___
9.	a) 1, b) 3, c) 2	___
10.	a) 3, b) 2, c) 1	___
11.	a) 1, b) 2, c) 3	___
12.	a) 2, b) 3, c) 1	___

TOTAL: ___

12–19: You seem, at the moment, to be too individualistic to be either leader or follower, committed rather to your own somewhat leisurely agenda. There is no reason why you should not prove a leader should you desire it, but first you must find a *milieu* about which you care. You seem laid back if kind and confident. Perhaps your heart is not in your work, and you should be considering a change of direction. Remember that your experience will be of value in whatever field you aspire to. Not all of us need a cause to which to adhere with passion. Drifting has its attractions. If, however, you have not the wealth or the talent to be your own boss, and want work that will motivate you, it is time for a change.

20–27: You seem to be leadership material, able at once to understand – and withstand – your subordinates, potential or otherwise, and to delegate work to them. Leadership is at once to do with autonomy, a strong sense of identity and purpose, empathy and, perhaps above all, the ability to manage time. At the same time, natural leaders are not control-freaks, interfering with their employees' independence, creativity or eccentricity, but enable all concerned to fulfill their potential, while retaining control of things like family and capital – the actual. They keep the rules writ in water – constantly changing according to circumstance – not least because it keeps others on their toes. They are ferocious only on behalf of their followers and dependents – not themselves – and, because they must have vision, they know the need for silence. An artist can be as sympathetic and impulsive as he will. It hurts no one but himself. A leader must be sympathetic, impulsive and able to dissociate himself, after due consideration, from such individuality where necessary. He must speak – and hear – many voices at once, and distinguish between their pleas.

28–36. Oh, how busy you must be, how preoccupied, how devoted to doing the Right Thing. These are the traits of a dedicated follower. Leaders do not give a damn about doing the Right Thing, except in so far as it affects other productive people about them. As a follower or functionary, you will thrive, and a good follower is anything but a loser. You are conscientious and hard-working and take what you do seriously; your ambition is to excel at your job, not to fly too high and melt your wings. It is probably wise, for the sake of your health and your associates, to ease up a little, to smell the roses and to consider what your life is for, where you are bound, and how you can expand your horizons.

Are you making the most of yourself at work?

```
 1.  a) 1,  b) 2,  c) 3   ___
 2.  a) 1,  b) 3,  c) 2   ___
 3.  a) 2,  b) 1,  c) 3   ___
 4.  a) 1,  b) 3,  c) 3   ___
 5.  a) 1,  b) 2,  c) 3   ___
 6.  a) 2,  b) 1,  c) 3   ___
 7.  a) 3,  b) 1,  c) 2   ___
 8.  a) 2,  b) 1,  c) 3   ___
 9.  a) 2,  b) 1,  c) 3   ___
10.  a) 1,  b) 3,  c) 2   ___
11.  a) 3,  b) 2,  c) 1   ___
12.  a) 3,  b) 1,  c) 2   ___

TOTAL:                    ___
```

12–19: Whatever else you may be, you are not a team-worker, and your aggression seems to argue a degree of self-absorption incompatible with good management either of your own emotions or, in consequence, of anyone else's. Take time out to talk to others in the workplace, to consider their insecurities in relation to your own, and above all to listen to and to tell stories. We are all of us translating all the time. Each of us has different fears, associations, histories, home environments etc. Even a simple word such as "dog," for example, will evoke different responses and will conjure different pictures in different people. How much more, then, will we fail to relate when we use vague or abstract terms? If you feel lousy for any reason, find an amusing and vivid way in which to describe the feeling. If envy, resentment or frustration possess you, find a parable to which others can relate. If someone else is distressed, try to recall an occasion on which you were similarly afflicted, and how you pulled yourself out of the condition. Keep it light, make fun of yourself. You will, astonishingly, grow in power by doing so and find it infinitely easier to motivate your subordinates and peers.

20–27: Words like "stubborn," "officious" and "interfering" spring to mind. You would seem to be the sort of person who thinks of him or herself as industrious, efficient management caliber, but has not yet succeeded in persuading anyone else of your leadership qualities. This is a trap into which so many people seem to fall, both in industry and in the home. You are not embattled. You have as good a chance as the next man or woman to introduce creative thinking and teamwork into the workplace and to get things done. Remember, it is not the highly qualified, humorless whiz-kid who gets to the top, but the person who knows how to motivate others, to make light of troubles and to empathize. You cannot begin to do this if you cling to your dignity and your position as if your life depended on it. Ease up a bit. Ask advice. Share your experience with others. Encourage group decisions. Woo your peers and subordinates rather than your bosses.

28–36: You plainly enjoy your work and are ready to consult with others working with you. When once people trust you, they will follow your lead, but they can only trust you if your principles and your position are confidently held.

Is your relationship in danger of "flooding"?

```
 1.  a) 1,  b) 2,  c) 3   ___
 2.  a) 1,  b) 2,  c) 3   ___
 3.  a) 3,  b) 1,  c) 2   ___
 4.  a) 1,  b) 3,  c) 2   ___
 5.  a) 3,  b) 2,  c) 1   ___
 6.  a) 1,  b) 3,  c) 2   ___
 7.  a) 1,  b) 2,  c) 3   ___
 8.  a) 2,  b) 1,  c) 3   ___
 9.  a) 2,  b) 1,  c) 3   ___
10.  a) 3,  b) 1,  c) 2   ___
11.  a) 1,  b) 2,  c) 3   ___
12.  a) 1,  b) 3,  c) 2   ___
```

TOTAL: ___

12–19: There are two words which the emotionally intelligent should excise from their vocabulary because they are dangerous, destructive lies. They are "always" and "never." No one is always or never anything. People have irritating habits, destructive vices, bad traits which surface from time to time, insecurities which manifest themselves as assertiveness, fears which emerge disguised as certainties, prejudices founded on ignorance, but they are people, not monsters, for all that. "Always" and "never" turn criticisms: "That is a thoughtless act" into insults – "You are always thoughtless"; and insults, because they cannot be answered with reason, are nothing short of violence, which breeds violence in its turn. "Always" and "never" do violence to the person who thinks and speaks such nonsense, because, in time, he or she begins to believe it, and his or her head becomes crowded with mythological monsters. Your responses – even to overtures of peace and acts of kindness – are pre-programmed to fight-or-flight. It may be too late for you to banish these lies, but, if your relationship is worth saving – and most are, in one form or another – list your partner's qualities and praise them, remind yourself of all the reasons that you got together in the first place, count your blessings and gently communicate your distress. Be ready to say "sorry" and to make concessions over trivial matters. Develop a code, for your own purposes or, if possible, to be shared with your partner, in order to identify upsurges of irritation, anger or panic. Break the cycle by recognizing that you are both badly bruised and need to be handled very, very gently . . .

20–27: The illusions of "always" and "never," detailed above, often result from disappointment at *dis*illusion. The notion that your lover is perfect, wonderful, marvellous and superhuman is natural in the first emotional deluge called "falling in love," but it is nonetheless untrue for that, and each subsequent, inevitable disillusion is seen, unjustly, as a betrayal. Romance is just that – romancing, or telling stories – and, on its own, a poor basis for a relationship. Love is lovely – make the most of it – but recognize that, the more you idealize, the more bitter and cruel will be the adaptation to reality. It is easy to love a fictional character, a lot harder to muddle along with a fellow human.

28–36: There is no danger of flooding here – merely, perhaps, of complacency – but at least you can choose to inject gallantry, comedy, games and romance into your relationship when you will, without feeling that, by doing so, you are making a concession.